Woman, Don't Die

Woman, Don't Die

Stephanie White

Woman, Don't Die
Stephanie White

Published By:
KPGM Book Publishers
(a division of Kingdom Publishing Group, Inc.)
P.O. Box 3273. Henrico, VA 23228
www.kingdompublishing.org

Library of Congress

ISBN 13: 978-0-9833651-4-3

Cover Design by: Matthew Williams, Sr.

"Woman, Don't Die"

Woman the day has come; when time is revealed,
The point of knowing that God has you near.
The storms of life once brought this Woman down,
But thank God for His love and mercy, she has found.
She pours her love into her friends and family,
With the joy of the Lord, He gives to her so freely,
Woman, when you thought you had, had enough,
The angel of God whispers, "Don't give up."
Woman you have a divine destiny that you have to see
If only you will trust Him and believe.

Acknowledgements

Thank you to my family and friends, for your support and words of encouragement throughout this journey. I extend a special thank you to the members of "Kingdom Business Ministry," for your faithfulness and dedication.

I must give all thanks to the one and only Almighty God, who is the head of my life. Thank You, God, for everything You have done in my life.

To God Be The Glory! Nothing can be done without Him.

Table of Contents

Preface

We, as believers, are called to draw the lost into the body of Christ. The Bible speaks, "He who wins souls is wise." Question: If you are a Christian, have any souls been won through your light? If you answer, "No," then I advise you to check your light switch, because it may be off, or you may just be disconnected from the Light Source who is Christ Jesus—The Light of the world.

If you are not a believer, have you done anything good to help or change someone else's life? If not, think about this: What if the people, who did good for you in your life, had not done so? Where would you be, or better yet, what would you be if they had not decided to help you?

Woman Don't Die is the testimony of someone who endured much in life. The purpose of this book is not to preach at you or to give scripture after scripture. If that were so, then why would you need to read this book? You could just pick up the Bible and read it. Alternatively, the purpose is to inspire others to hold on to the Master's (God's) unchanging hand. When you want to give up, or when people have betrayed you, do not let go.

Many times in my life I wanted to give up, but God! He kept me when I could not keep myself. My desire is to help change someone else's life; and to encourage them to have faith in God, or to increase their faith in Him even more.

Woman, Don't Die purposes to encourage people of all nationalities and genders. Although the story is shared from a woman's perspective, all, both men and women, can benefit from knowing that when all else fails, God is still in the midst.

Woman, Don't Die shares the story of a single mother raising her two children. Loraine Peterson is a woman whose faith is challenged in trying times, yet she insists on teaching her children Godly values in the midst of complicated situations. Some of Loraine's choices have severe consequences; not just for her, but for her children as well. The things she endures forces her to continually ask the question, *"When the pressures of life are pounding you, who do you turn too?"*

There may be times in your life when it seems as though everything has crumbled and everyone has betrayed you. It may seem as if no one is there when you need them. When this occurs, you must know that no matter what, God has you covered.

As a Pastor and author, my mission is to reach those "Loraine Peterson's" around the world. I want to persuade them to turn to God and hold on to Him. I want encourage them as I shout, **Woman, Don't Die!**

Choices

"The choices you make in life can affect the people who are connected to you."

~ Choices ~

Have you ever found yourself asking the question, "Why me?" In life, we sometimes find ourselves at the door of choices. The choice that we make could be easy or critical for us. Life has a way of bringing people in our environment that may be there for a season or a lifetime. We must know that we have the power to determine how long they will stay. We can decide whether or not we want them to be a part of our life. The choices we make establish our path for our present, and future. Proverbs 3:5-6 says, "Trust in the Lord with all your heart; and lean not unto your own understanding. In all your ways acknowledge him and he shall direct your paths." If we get out of our flesh and stop trying to figure things out on our own, then maybe our paths would be a little smoother. We must stop and ask for direction from our Lord, who is ruler over our life.

Meet Loraine Peterson

There is someone I would like to introduce to you. Her name is Loraine Peterson. Loraine is a very tall woman with sandy brown, curly hair. Her skin tone is that of smooth caramel, with no blemishes. She has eyes that slant upward, as if someone had braided her hair too tight.

Loraine was the average preacher's kid (PK). She was raised in the church by her father, a deacon, and she always had a strong belief in God. Even though they went to church, they still had their struggles.

Loraine's mother was not the supportive, outgoing mother you would imagine. Mrs. Peterson was a very stout, light-skinned woman, who wore a close-cut hairstyle. She always had an expression of hurt on her face. This was probably due to her feeling that her husband loved Loraine more than her. She could never accept the fact that her husband could love an adopted child so much.

When she was sixteen, Loraine met this guy as he passed by near the corner store. He was about 5'2" tall, with a dark chocolate complexion, hazel eyes, and coal black wavy hair. He was built like Arnold Schwarzenegger but in a smaller package. Larry was the bad boy who all the girls wanted. When she returned to school, Loraine saw him again for the second time, but this time he saw her too. As time went by, she chose to creep around with him. This went on for months.

Loraine knew that her father would never approve of Larry. One day, it was too late. She became pregnant and her faith would not allow her to get rid of the baby. She was forced to introduce Larry to her father and mother. She told them her situation while Larry stood in the living room with her. Mr. Peterson slowly got up out of the chair and went into the bedroom. Never looking back at Loraine, he slowly closed the door. Mrs. Peterson stood in front of Loraine, staring her directly in the eyes and said, "I knew one day you would break his heart, but I did not know it would be this soon. Get out and get out now!" Loraine screamed, "Where will I go!? What do I do!? What do I do!?" Her mother gripped her by the arm and shoved her out of the door and said, "I don't know, but it is not our problem! "Sit the bastard in the streets, I don't care!"

Larry told Loraine she could stay with him and his brother at their apartment. Loraine's eyes were filled with tears of disappointment and pain.

Pain

"And God shall wipe away all tears from their eyes; and there shall be no more death, neither sorrow, nor crying, neither shall there be any more pain...." (Revelation 21:4 KJV).

~ Pain ~

Years pass by and Loraine has not heard from her parents since that dreadful day. She and Larry, Sr. married a year after the incident and now have two children, Larry, Jr. and Kimmie. Loraine finished her GED and is now in nursing school. To earn extra money, she works two part-time jobs: one at the hospital and the other in housekeeping. Larry Sr. is a general contractor. They are doing very well for themselves as a family. Even though, they had their ups and downs, they are still holding on to their marriage.

The first two years of their marriage were very difficult, because of Larry Sr. drinking and staying out late at night. Loraine stayed with him because she had no where to go to get away from the mental and physical abuse. Within the first year of their marriage, Loraine saw another side of Larry, Sr.

One night, he came home when Loraine and the children were in the bed. Sweaty, smelly and drunk, Larry, Sr. staggered into their bedroom. He started kicking Loraine and striking her several times on her face with a half-filled beer bottle. He poured beer all over her, wrapped her long hair around his hand and began dragging her out of the bed and into the streets with just a t-shirt on in the pouring down rain. When Larry, Jr. ran out to help his mother, Larry, Sr. back-handed him across the face, knocking him onto the ground.

The next morning, Larry, Sr. came into the kitchen. Loraine, Kimmie, and Larry, Jr. were sitting at the table eating their breakfast. Larry, Sr. came into the kitchen, apologized to her and the children, kissed Loraine on her forehead, picked up his hardhat and lunch and walked out the door. Loraine lifted her head, displaying the black and purple bruises around her eyes. She was in such crucial pain that she could hardly move to prepare the children for school. He promised to never hit her or the children ever again, but many times after, it happened., again.

Loraine left home to go to her housekeeping job for a few hours, but realized she did not have to work so she returned home. Larry, Sr. was at home with the children for the day. As she arrived home from work, the music was so loud she could hear it as she was driving around the corner. Kimmie and Larry, Jr. were playing in the front yard, listening to the music coming from the house. Loraine wondered why the music was so loud. She noticed a sporty two-door red convertible parked across the street. She had never seen that car before. As she reached to turn the music down, she heard noises coming from her bedroom. Loraine called out for Larry, Sr. but there was no response from him. The closer and closer she approached her bedroom, she could hear the noises increase. The door was shut. She pushed the door open with the palm of her hand. There was Larry, Sr. lying in the bed with his arms folded behind his head and eyes closed. Loraine shouted out to Larry, Sr., "Get up!" At first, she did not see the figure moving beside him, under the covers. She slowly walked toward the bed. Larry, Sr. eased up from under the covers with his eyes wide open as though he saw a ghost. The figure stopped moving and Loraine slowly gripped the covers, then pulled them back. She immediately stumbled back against the wall and slid down as though she had melted. Larry, Sr. told her to get out the room. She screamed, "Larry, Sr. a man!!! What have you done?" Screaming and trembling, she said, "Why? What have I done to deserve this?"

Larry, Sr. looked at Loraine and told her to get out! The man was searching for his clothes to leave saying, "I am so sorry Mrs. Peterson. Larry, call me later. This is too much drama for me!" Larry Sr. told him, "You don't have to leave; she's going." Loraine leaned back with a surprised look as though someone had waxed her eyebrows like the McDonald's arch. Loraine snatched her purse, got her children, hopped into her car, and left. As she drove down the road shaking, she pulled over and asked God, "Why me?" While the tears rolled down her cheeks, she picked up her cell phone and called her parents. Her mother answered.

With tears flowing down her face and sniffling uncontrollably, Loraine asked how they were doing. Her mother informed her that her father died four months earlier. Before Loraine could ask if she and the children could stay a few days, her mother hung up the phone. Her heart just stopped, she felt a cold chill go all over her body.

Loraine decided to call one of her friends from the church she had been attending. Sister Vanessa was a nice figured, Latino woman who was beautiful, sassy and well-educated. However, she struggled with her identity and used her beauty to compensate for what she lacked in other areas. Sister Vanessa told Loraine that she and the children could stay with her and her husband, Bryan, for awhile.

Bryan was a high-class attorney who was extremely wealthy and exceptionally good looking. Bryan was controlling and quite demanding of Sister Vanessa.

Loraine and Vanessa became very close over the years, while being members of St. Thomas Baptist Pentecostal Church of Deliverance. Vanessa shared with Loraine that her healing would come in time.

Time

"A time to love, and a time to hate; a time of war, and a time of peace" (Ecclesiastes 3:8 KLV).

~ Time ~

Time has taken its course. Loraine now has an apartment of her own with her two children, who are now grown up. Loraine finished nursing school and now works full-time at the hospital.

It was a rainy afternoon when Loraine arrived home from her job at the hospital. She worked a double shift because the hospital was short of staff so she decided to take a nap before the children came home. Nobody was home, so she went into the kitchen to prepare something for dinner. The phone rang and it was Larry, Sr. complaining about child support. He had been informed that he had to appear in court on Monday morning for an increase in his child support payments. Loraine was upset because he was behind over $14,000.00 in child support.

Ring. Ring. Ring. "Hello?" said Loraine. "What is this about appearing in court for more money, Loraine?" asked Larry, Sr. "Look, when was the last time you sent any money or came by to see the kids, Sherlock Holmes! Try paying something so your payments won't build up." barked Loraine.

"Give me a break woman," said Larry Sr. "Hey! I do not have the time to entertain you about your problems. Try making your payments on time. Oh, ask your friend how's it hanging!" (Click) She hung the phone up on him.

The door opened and it was her daughter, Kimmie, with the biggest, brightest smile on her face. "Hi mom, what is today?" She was coming from school. She took off her coat and slowly laid it on the couch. Loraine was silent. "Who is the birthday girl?" asked Kimmie. "Who is the birthday girl?" asked Loraine? Kimmie approached her mother standing in the kitchen, looking in the refrigerator. Kimmie grabs her mom around the waste with a smile. "Mom, you know I want to have a birthday party at Lisa's house."

Loraine turned around and looked at her with a squint in one eye. "That won't happen! And why not here so I can keep an eye on you girls?" she asked, as she continued preparing for dinner. Mom! Loraine replied, "Okay, who is supposed to be at this so-called party?" "Just us girls and a few guys, Heeey!" joked Kimmie. "You know I am a woman of God, so I am not condoning such a thing. Oh no! Just you and the girls with some guys, Yeah right!" said Loraine. This is my eighteenth birthday mom, please? I will be legally grown! And plus, you are saved mom, not me! I want to have my party." "You must have lost your everlasting mind girl!" Yelled

Lorraine. "You will not have a rump shacking, booty drop like it's a hot party. As a matter of fact, since you cannot tell the difference between me and your friends when you are talking to me, how about you are grounded for two weeks, Miss!" Kimmie yelled back, "I want to have my party!" While Loraine and Kimmie argued about the birthday party, Larry, Jr. entered the house. Larry, Jr. was trying to find out what was going on. Why was his baby sister arguing with their mother? He walked into the kitchen with them. There was screaming, shouting, banging of pots, and pans. Loraine threw her hands up and walked out of the kitchen; into the living room with tears in her eyes.

Suddenly, the house got quiet and nobody moved as Loraine began to pray to God about her children. She prayed her prayer, "Making it with Jesus." "The pressure of life is weighing me down. I just can't seem to come around, but Jesus, I know you will never let me down."

Deception

**"And Jesus answered and said unto them,
Take heed that no man deceive you"
(Matthew 24:4 KJV).**

~ Deception ~

Kimmie was sitting at the kitchen table doing her homework. Then, there was a knock at the door. "Girl, open the door, it's me." It was Lisa, Kimmie's best friend since middle school. Lisa was a silent type friend, she had hair that was shiny yellow like the sun and her eyes matched the blue skies, as though they blended together. Lisa was calm but had a funny personality with an African American swagger. Kimmie asked, "Hey girl, what's up? Where are you coming from?" "I just came from the store where I saw Theresa and her man, Tyler. Theresa is one of Kimmie's friends but she only knew Theresa about six months. Theresa is a fast girl and cunning, but she has plenty of street smarts. She is not as fortunate as Lisa and Kimmie. Her mom is never around and she has to provide for herself. Kimmie and Lisa still befriended her regardless of her short comings. Theresa and Tyler are incredibly close because of their connections in the streets.

Tyler is the neighborhood thug who controlled the street blocks from First Street to One Hundred and Twenty-Fifth Street. He was the type that did everything illegal: Gang Banging,

Pimping, Gun Trade, Drug Deals and Car Chopping he did it all. He was so powerful that he had big time lawyers in his pocket and nothing got done unless he said so. Tyler began his criminal lifestyle at the age of fourteen. His mom was an elementary school teacher who fell in love with a big time drug dealer who later had her strung out on dope and prostituting. It did not take long before he was put into prison for life.

Tyler's dad was betrayed by his brother. Tyler has no trust in nobody but himself. Girl, I do not know how she puts up with him after all the stuff he be doing." Kimmie replied, "Yeah, I know. He is so trifling; I cannot stand him. Theresa knows about his so-called girls and selling dope. I don't understand why she is with him anyway. Oh, I don't have time to worry about her and her man. I need to figure out how I can have this party without my mom finding out."

Lisa asked Kimmie if she was still going to have her birthday party. "What? You're not going to have your party? Girl, oh we got to find a way. Kimmie, you know that you and Shawn are supposed to hook up. You told him it was going to happen at the party. Girl, he is too cute to keep being strung along. Somebody else been done grabbed him. You better watch yourself!" Kimmie replied, "Tell me something that I don't know." As they were talking, there was another knock at the door. 'Knock. Knock.' "Who is it?" Kimmie hollered at the door. It was Theresa, came in shaking her hips side-to-side, wearing her royal blue micro-mini skirt on. "Hey, what y'all doing?" asked Theresa. "Lisa, did I see you at the store on the corner of 5th and 6th street today?" "Yes and what were you and your man doing on the corner?" Theresa replied, "First of all, change your tone, and secondly, me and Tyler are just friends. We only have history together. Forget all that, so what about the party?" "My mama is tripping, girl." said Kimmie. "She can't have it and she is grounded not one, but two weeks," Lisa replied. "I think she's a little too old to be grounded, but that's between her and her mama," stated Lisa. "Kimmie, you know what's supposed to happen with you and Shawn at the party. Girl, he ain't going to keep waiting on you. Shoot, I been done snatched him up myself, okay?" said Theresa! "Look, I have an idea. I will have my mom to call your mom and tell her that she will be home doing the party at my house." "How is this supposed to work," asked Kimmie? "I will just give her some of her special candy from Tyler and it's on girl," Theresa began to laugh. All three of the girls were sitting around the table laughing and whispering. Then Larry, Jr. came out of the bathroom with only a towel on, dripping wet. He walked up to Kimmie and asked her, "Where is my blue t-shirt you keep using without my permission, Kimmie?"

Larry, Jr. glanced back at Lisa as she stared at him, slowly sliding her eyes up from his firm, 12-inch feet, his strong legs, his thick caramel thighs, and the towel fitting tightly around his apple bottom. He had water dripping onto his six pack from his chest like ripples of clear water on rocks in a stream on a cool summer's day. Lisa said, "Whoa! He is so fine! Come to mama, you Twix candy bar. With all that good looking chocolate on the outside, I know there is some sweet filling in the inside! Kimmie, your brother has got to be my baby's daddy." Theresa then informed Lisa that Larry, Jr. was going to be her man. Bending across the table, Theresa responded, "I don't think so. He is my future husband," waving her finger side to side in Lisa's face. Larry, Jr. went into his room and closed the door. "Don't either one of you even try it. And Theresa, you already have a man. Come on let's go to your house."

Anger

"The Lord is merciful and gracious, slow to anger and plenteous in mercy" (Psalms 103:8 KJV).

~ Anger ~

Loraine returned home from a long walk and Larry, Jr. was getting dressed to go to the community center to work out. He heard the door open and shut. Larry, Jr. asked, "Mom, that's you?" "Yes, baby, it's me." He walked toward his mother; hugged and kissed her on the cheek. "I am heading out to the community center. You want to come? You know you need to work off those love handles." "Boy, that is the best part. The man has to have something to hold on to. I am a size nine and physically fit, pretty boy," said Loraine as she reached to pinch his cheeks. "Little Larry, I have church tonight and Pastor Love is picking me up. I have to get those tires fixed on my car before people start to talk. Where is Kimmie?" asked Loraine. "She is over at Theresa's house." "She has changed since she started hanging around that girl, but I cannot blame her. Kimmie has a mind of her own. I pray that God will touch her and that she would just open her eyes to reality. People do not understand being in the wrong place at the wrong time can change a person's whole life. Well I am going to get dressed."

Loraine was in and out of her bedroom preparing for church. 'Ring. Ring. Ring.' Larry, Jr. answered the phone, "Hello." It was Pastor Love telling him to let Loraine know he was on his way in a few minutes. "Ok," Larry, Jr. replied. He shouted out of the living room, "Mom, Pastor Love is on his way in a few minutes."

Pastor Love is about one hundred and seventy-five pounds, slim, six feet tall, has black, silk wavy hair--cut close and jet black skin with a smile as bright as the morning sun. Pastor Love shared with Loraine in many counseling sessions that as long as she stayed focused on God, everything would work out for her. He cares about Loraine and her children. He helped Loraine get through some of the most difficult and trying times of her life.

Larry, Jr. let his mother know that he was about to leave and that she needed to listen out for Pastor Love at the door. "I am leaving to go to the community center," he yelled,. As he opened the door to leave, his father, Larry, Sr., was standing there, with his fist in the air, about to knock at the door. Larry, Sr. spoke to Larry Jr., but his son did not reply to his father. Larry, Jr. yelled to Loraine, "Your ex-husband is in the house." Larry, Sr. tried to talk with his son and explain to him his absence. Larry, Jr. asked him to leave while calling Loraine at the same time. Larry, Sr. says, "Hi, son. How is your sister? I really miss you and her. I am sorry about everything. I want to ..." He is cut off by Larry, Jr. and the door slams. Stop! What?! Why you here, man? I know you are sorry and that's why you mean nothing to me, so leave!"

There is a knock at the door. It is Pastor Love, dressed in a blue pin-stripped, three piece Armani suit, with shiny black Stacey Adams shoes, and a black top hat. Pastor Love is a single man of God and he pastors one of the largest churches in Chicago, Illinois. Pastor Love shared with Loraine in many counseling sessions that as long as she stayed focused on God, everything would work out. He cares so much about Loraine and her family. He helped Loraine get through some of her most difficult and trying times of her life.

Larry, Jr. welcomed Pastor Love into their home. "Hi, Pastor Love. I am out of here," he said, slamming the door behind him!. Pastor Love greeted Larry, Sr., while bending over to take off his hat. "My name is Pastor Love. Is Loraine ready?" Larry, Sr. began to question Pastor Love about his visit with Loraine. "Why are you here? Are you and Loraine supposed to be dating or what?" Larry, Sr. stood there staring at Pastor Love with those hazel eyes and hair slicked back into a ponytail as long as a rose bush. He was built like a body builder. Pastor Love replied, "That would be for Loraine to discuss with you." Larry, Sr. said, "See, I am her ex-husband if you did not know. I was her first boyfriend, her first man, and her first love. Hey, I was her first everything. You know what I mean?" Larry, Sr. smiled and rubbed his hands together as he looked up at Pastor Love. Pastor Love responded,

"See, I know Loraine is a wonderful woman. She is very hard working and quite lovely as well. She is a big girl and can handle anything that comes her way. This should not be too hard to believe. She is such a special woman because she overcame you, her ex-husband, and her ex-problem. A real man knows how to minister to a woman through her mind, emotions and needs. Oh, but you would not know that which is why you are her ex." Loraine calls out to Pastor Love, "I am on my way out of this room Pastor just give me a second please." She then yells, Larry, Sr., you need to leave because I have nothing more to talk to you about, so go!"

Loraine then heads out of her bedroom wearing a dazzling red dress that exposed her gorgeous shape. Her dark, sandy brown, curly hair was hanging down past her shoulders and swayed freely as she moved. To top it all off, her hot red and black stiletto heels amply supported her five-feet eight inch height.

Again, Loraine asked Larry, Sr. to leave. Larry, Sr. asked, "Is this where my money has been going—to the Pastor's pockets? And it looks like he is getting a little extra. Doesn't he get enough from the tithes and offerings of his members? You're supposed to be a woman of God, always preaching.

Look at you in that tight red dress. You better stop this child support increase, baby girl!" "What? Larry! And what are you going to do if I don't? Beat me? Kick me? Or drag me? What? What?!" Lorraine, overflowing with anger, remembered the things he put her through. "Nothing but pay. Now get out of my apartment before I call the cops! Bye!" She shoved him out and slammed the door in his face. Shouting through the door, Larry stated, "Don't worry, I am out! But I will be back to settle this situation," he said, balling his fist tightly in his hand.

Loraine turned to Pastor Love, "I apologize for the drama. He can be a pain at times. Well, You are looking good, Mr. GQ."

"Yes I do, don't I? Sister Loraine Peterson, you look breath-taking. Seeing you in that red dress is like the apple of any man's eye. A view of delight." "Thank you, Pastor Love." blushed Loraine. "Are you ready? Let's roll."

Lustful Thoughts

"This I say then, Walk in the Spirit, and ye shall not fulfill the lust of the flesh" (Galatians 5:16 KJV).

~ Lustful Thoughts ~

Pastor Love opened the car door of his navy blue sporty Jaguar for Lorraine. She reached over and unlocked the door for him. As they were riding in the car, Pastor Love realized that Loraine's seat belt was not on. "Loraine, your seatbelt is not on. May I?" "Surely you may," replied Loraine. He slowly leaned over, pulled her seatbelt across her, and fastened her belt tightly. Pastor Love asked Loraine, "Are you cold?" "A little," replied Loraine. "Let me turn the heat on for a while," said Pastor Love. "Loraine, I have to say that red dress looks amazing on you." Loraine *(Thinking to herself), And you, Mr. Love, don't look bad yourself. Please Lord forgive me. It's been ten years and he just smells and looks so good. (She is thinking) I know he just did not slide that seatbelt across me. I am going to have to stop riding with Pastor Love, because he is about to get a whole lot of love! Come back Loraine, that's not going to happen. I need some help, badly. Lord, keep me.* While Loraine is thinking to herself she is repenting the whole time.

They soon arrived at the church. "We are here," announced Pastor Love. They arrived at the brick building 250ft wide and 75ft high church with a 4-foot steeple. The sign read, St. Thomas Baptist Pentecostal Church of Deliverance. The lights around the church's parking lot were as bright as the moonlight on a clear night. "If you need a ride to Bible Study just give me a call Loraine. I mean it." (He smiles, staring at her) "Okay," said Loraine. "and thank you for the ride, Pastor Love." *(she is thinking)* If he smiles at me again I am going to need more prayer.

One of the deacons met them by the church's front door and opened the door for Loraine. Pastor Love went one way, and Loraine was greeted by sister Vanessa Staples. As they walked into the church, she informed Loraine of the rumors about her riding with Pastor Love the last few days and why she did not show up for choir rehearsal. "Loraine, girl watch yourself. People are talking." "I do not care what people think. You should know that after what happen with Larry, Sr. People do not matter; especially when I have not done anything. Plus, Pastor Love is not interested in a single mom with two kids and a stupid ex-husband." Loraine tells her about the argument with Larry, Sr. and Kimmie. "Don't you know that fool had the nerve to question Pastor Love about why he was picking me up?" "No he didn't," replied Vanessa. "That's not all. Kimmie wanted to have a party with just her and a few guys. I told her no. We argued and I punished her for two weeks. Girl, you be having too much drama for me," said Vanessa. "Don't even try it. I have children and ex-problems. You have crazy husband ones," said Loraine.

The usher whispered to them, "Please be quiet the service is about to begin." Pastor Love came out into the pulpit and began to preach on hurting people and how God will hold it together until we get it together. "That man is so fine," said Vanessa. "I know girl. All that time he never ever, never ever tried anything while you road with him?" "Well, well he fastened my seatbelt. Does that count for anything?" asked Loraine. "Um, no! It's just the law or maybe he did not want you to fall out. Who knows?

The church was pack with twenty-five hundred people, many of whom were shouting and dancing in the aisles. The choir sang like angels, on one accord. Loraine stood up with her hands stretched wide open in the air asking God to watch over her family and to clean her heart from lustful thoughts about Pastor Love. "Lord, help me to stop thinking lustful thoughts about this man."

Sowing

**"How does one profit from reaping,
unless the seed has been sown?"**

~ Sowing ~

Kimmie was about to leave Theresa's house. (She is talking and putting on her coat while walking toward the door.) Theresa reminds Kimmie that her mother will ask her mother when she gets home from church. "Mom, I need you to call Kimmie's mom and ask her about her party being here. Also, make sure you tell her you will be here." "Okay!" replies her mom. "Oh yeah, here, take this." Theresa takes a round milky white hard substance and puts it into the palm of her mother's hand and closes it. Theresa's mom agrees with the plan and calls Kimmie's mom.

"Hello Loraine. Is it okay if Kimmie has her party over here? I will be home." Loraine is not too sure about it, but agreed so that she won't have to argue with Kimmie anymore. "Well, I guess it will be okay. Are you sure you are going to be there? I am kind of shaky about this party, but okay," said Loraine. Theresa's mom informed her that Kimmie's mom has agreed to have the party. Theresa said the party was going to start at ten and the news was out. "Well, I have to go and get ready for my part'ay. It's going to be on." Dancing and laughing, she walks around the corner.

Kimmie was out the door and down the road on her way home to pick out her outfit for the party, when she runs into Tyler. Tyler calls her over and asks her questions about the party. "Yo shorty! What's up? Come here, I heard about the party am I invited?" Loraine told him that he nor his friends were invited. Tyler laughed at her and informed her that he calls the shouts at Theresa's house. "Let me hip you to my world, shorty. Whatever goes on in that house, I allow it. Nothing happens unless I say it happens, you got it?" *(pointing his finger at her as he walked toward her)* "If you want to still have that party, you better watch yourself, pretty girl." Tyler then begins to approach her to grab her. She was near the corner where the community center was. Larry, Jr. was coming out of the building. He ran up and jumped in between both of them. Facing Tyler, he yelled, "Hey! Don't you put your hands on my sister man. Do you hear me?" (Yelling in Tyler's face and pointing his finger in his face) said Larry Jr. (Asking Tyler to stay away from his sister) "You don't know that you are as close as my nose is from my face to death little man," Tyler replied. (His friends snatched guns out and pointed them at Larry, Jr.) "You can still have your party if you want shorty. But you, I will see again. Peace Out!" (He held his arms stretched out in front of his three friends, slowly walking away).

Larry, Jr. and Kimmie walked and talked as they went up the steps to their home. "Kimmie, why do you hang around these people? Baby sis, don't have that party. Wake up." (They are walked up the steps of their Chicago brick apartment complex, connected to twenty other apartments). "Tyler, do not scare me with his Niño Brown, New Jack City want'a be self." *She stood on the top steps, as her brother was on the bottom step below. She looked her brother in the face).* "Nothing is going to stop me from having my party; him, mama or a Hurricane. I mean nothing!" Loraine was at home and tells Kimmie she could have her party as long as Theresa's mother was going to be there. "Hi kids," states Lorraine. "Kimmie, Theresa's mom called me about the party. I told her that as long as she was there, it would be okay. Please, Kimmie I am trying to trust you. Don't let me down." "Thanks mom, I wont."

Kimmie was excited and began to pick out her clothes. Larry, Jr. was not too happy about his mother's decision and was still a little upset about the incident with his father. "Mom, why are you going to let her have this party?" "I made this decision," said Loraine. "So let me be the parent here alright? I have to get ready for work tonight," replied Loraine. "Well, you all do what you want. You, Kimmie, and dad are not going to worry me!" Larry, Jr. was angry with everyone. He exited out the door with hurt in his eyes.

Reaping

"He who sows iniquity will reap calamity and futility and the rod of his wrath with which he smites others will fail" (Proverbs 22:8 AMP).

~ Reaping ~

The wind was blowing and whistling around like dancers in a Broadway musical. Paper, leaves and Loraine's scarf all flowed in the night air. It was as cold as icicles, hanging frozen from a weeping tree. Loraine walked to work with the wind pressed against her back. She felt that something was not right with the choice she made, allowing her daughter to have that party. 'It is cold out here tonight,' she thought. 'My hands and feet are frozen. I just don't feel right in my spirit about this party.'

Loraine finally arrived at work. Her hands and feet felt like they were frostbitten. Now Kimmie had arrived at her party. People were standing around outside with beer cans in their hands and smoking. When she entered the house, the crowd was tight. She could barely get in because of the people blocking the doorway. "Hey! What's up y'all?" *(Waving her hands in the air from side to side)* "This is the party of the year. Man I can barely get in here. Excuse me, my peeps." Theresa spotted Kimmie and called her over. She had a beer in her hand and was laughing and singing happy birthday to

Kimmie. "Kimmie, over here! Girl what's up? Come and get one of these cold ones." *(She was singing)* "Happy birthday to yah, Happy birthday to yah, Happy birthday!" When Theresa came though the crowd, Tyler was behind her. He was staring Kimmie straight in the eye; the stare frightened her, but she brushed it off. "Happy birthday, shorty," said Tyler. "Thank you very much Tyler." "So where is your brother?" Tyler asked. "Why he's not here with his baby sis? Anything can happen on a night like this." Lisa comes and pulls Kimmie with her to the dance floor, pointing at Shawn. "Come on Kimmie, let's hit the floor girl." *(Lisa pulling her by the arm)* "Look at who's on the dance floor looking so fine. It's Shawn and he was looking for you." Let me show you how to do this dance, while I move over here by Mr. Smooth." She danced closer and closer toward Shawn.

Theresa passed Kimmie a drink while she was on the dance floor. Tyler was still staring at Kimmie afar off. Shawn approached Kimmie and they go off alone into one of Theresa's bedroom. "What's up shorty? You are looking fine tonight. Those jeans are fitting in all the right places. You know I have been trying to get with you for a long time baby girl. How about us going into one of these rooms and get to know each other little better?" asked Shawn. "Okay. Let's get this party started." Kimmie is feeling dizzy, but continues to go with him. Shawn noticed that something was wrong with her. He asked, "What's wrong baby girl?" "I feel weak, help." Kimmie begins to feel drowsy and weak, and then she passed out on the bed. "Baby girl, wake up! Baby girl wake up!" (He jumped up and opened the door wide and yelled for Lisa) "Man, this cannot be happening to me!" said Shawn. (Pacing back and forth shacking and trembling) "I did nothing!"

Shawn goes to tell Lisa what has happened to Kimmie and shuts the door behind him. The room was dark and Kimmie was in and out of this deep sleep, but she could not move. All she could say was "Lord, help me. What is going on with me?" and she passed out again.

Then, the door slowly opened and a shadow passed by the bed and stood in front of her. It was Tyler. He began to touch her softly on her arm and then snatches her shirt open. "Oh shorty, you thought you could handle me. I told you this is my house and I say what goes on up in here!" (He began to beating on his chest with his fist) "Let's see how high you can get shorty. This is the good stuff you are getting," he said, as he tied a rubber tube around her arm and injected her with drugs. "It will make you want to fly high into the sky." (He was laughing as he finished injecting her) "Your big brother is not here to protect you this time. I wonder what he will do with a junky for a sister." Tyler left the room and shut the door. Lisa passed Tyler as he was coming out of the room. She asked him, "What are you doing coming out of there Tyler?" She walked into the room and saw Kimmie on the bed. Lisa began screaming. "Help me! Help me!" Everyone came running to the door and Theresa pushed through the crowd. "Move back. Get out of my way! What is happening Lisa?" *(She is crying)* "What are we going to do? Where is your mom, Theresa?" Lisa was screaming at Theresa. "Let's get her to the hospital now!" (People were standing around, the music had stopped and people were crying.) Then Theresa started telling everyone to get out and told Lisa, "Let's get her to the hospital right now."

Loraine was in her office on the phone with Pastor Love, telling him about how she felt about letting Kimmie have her party. While she was on the phone, she heard on the intercom that a young lady was coming into the emergency room for rape and drugs. Lisa ran passed Loraine's office door, stopped, and turned around crying as she fell to her knees. Loraine asked her what was wrong. "Please talk to me." Lisa uttered out, "Kim' Kimmie." Then Theresa appeared behind Lisa with one tear coming down her face and a runny nose. Then she mumbles, "I am sorry Mrs. Peterson. I am so sorry." Loraine asked, "Where is Kimmie, Theresa?" (Theresa pointed into the emergency hallway.) Loraine pushed past the two girls and ran down the hall.

The doctor told her to wait and she asked them who the young lady was that went through the doors. Then Nurse Jones came out of the room and spoke to Loraine. She said, "It is Kimmie; she has been raped and injected with Heroin. The doctor is trying to clean her system with a drug that they use in these cases. They have run HIV and other STDs tests. Please Loraine, give us a chance to handle this situation to the best of our ability; you know the procedures." Loraine hit's the floor and screams. While she is there Larry, Jr. ran up with tears in his eyes. He shouts, "Mom, what's going on with Kimmie?" He grabbed Loraine and held her tight, rubbing her hair. While both of them were crying, Theresa and her mother came up and told Loraine how sorry they were. Loraine stood up and asked, "Where were you two when my daughter was being raped?" She looked both of them in the eyes and said "I knew I should have never trusted my child with either of you." Theresa's mom said, "Don't try to make this our problem. I can't help it if you cannot control your daughter!" Loraine turned and looked her straight in the eyes and slapped her. Theresa's mother fell to the wall. Her nose was bleeding. Theresa said, "Let's go mama."

Larry, Jr. asked Lisa what had happen at the party. When Lisa had told him what happened, Pastor Love entered the waiting area. Loraine was sitting down and as she looked up, he was standing over her. Pastor Love asked if Kimmie was going to be okay. She told him it had been four hours since they had heard anything.

Loraine's cell phone rang and it was Vanessa crying on the other end. She told Loraine that she was only minutes away. Then Larry, Sr. comes in through the emergency doors with his new friend. He asked Loraine, "How could you let something like this happen?" Larry, Jr. said, "We don't have time for this now dad, so sit down and wait like the rest of us."

Everyone was sitting and waiting to hear from the doctor when Vanessa and Brian arrived. With tears in her eyes, Vanessa said, "Loraine, I am so sorry this has happened." Pastor Love said, "Let us all hold hands and pray that God will work a miracle for Kimmie." The doctor came out and told everyone to go home for the night, because the tests would not be in until tomorrow. So everyone left the hospital, except for Pastor Love and Loraine. She asked if could she see her daughter and the doctor said it would be fine for a few minutes.

Pastor Love went in with Loraine. Kimmie was laying in the bed asleep. Loraine sat down beside her, and Pastor Love stood near her and they began to pray even the more.

Pressure

"Come unto me, all ye that labour and are heavy laden, and I will give you rest.. For my yoke is easy and my burdens are light."
Matthew 11:28, 30 KJV

~ Pressure ~

When Larry, Jr. woke up, he looked out of his window. It was a bright sunny morning. The birds were chirping and the winds had ceased. He went into Kimmie's room and she was not there. He left out of her room and entered into Loraine's room and found it was empty too. Larry, Jr. went into the bathroom to take a shower and while he was in there, the phone rang. He got out of the shower dripping wet. He answered, "Hello." It was Greg. He wanted to know what happened to Kimmie.

Greg is a volunteer at the community center where Larry, Jr. attends. He mentors the young men in the community. Larry, Jr. is very close to him; something like a father and son relationship. Larry, Jr. informed him he would explain to him when he came over. While Larry, Jr. was walking down the street, he met up with one of Tyler's homeboys. He started telling him what Tyler was bragging to him and some other guys about what happened. He felt that Tyler did Larry, Jr.'s sister wrong and that he should pay for it. Larry, Jr. was furious about what the guy had told him. How Tyler had planned it all out. At that time, Greg drove up in his yard and blew the horn at Larry, Jr. coming down the road.

Larry, Jr. walked up to Greg as he exited the car. Tears were rolling down Larry, Jr.'s face as he started to explain to Greg what the guy told him about Tyler. He stated that he is going to kill Tyler. "Man, I can't take this no more," Larry Jr. shouted out! Greg grabbed and hugged him and he said, "Don't think like that man, you are better than that." They entered into the house with their arms around each other. Greg asks Larry Jr. does he want anything to drink or to eat. So Larry Jr. told Greg everything that happened that night. Greg encouraged him to keep his head up and be strong for his mom and sister. The phone rang it was Greg's ex-wife asking what time he was going to drop off the alimony money. While Greg was on the phone, Larry Jr. fell asleep on Greg's black leather couch. He felt a touch on his shoulder it was Greg waking him up. "Hey man, it's late let's go check on your mom and sister." Larry Jr. said, "Not now. I just want to sit here for awhile to get my thoughts together." Greg said, "Okay, I'll be back later." Larry, Jr.'s cell phone rang. It was Pastor Love asking him where he was because his mom was looking for him. He told Pastor Love that he was at a friend's house. He asked, "How is my mom and sister, Pastor?" Pastor Love stated, "Your mom is okay, but your sister is still not responding." Pastor Love told Larry, Jr. he will keep in touch with the family and will continue to pray for them. Larry Jr. rolled over and a tear slid down his cheek. He fell back asleep and Greg entered the house and stood over him watching him.

Greg decided to catch a nap before work. He went in his room to get ready for work. While he was in the shower, the bathroom door opened. He looked and it was Larry, Jr. standing there watching him. Greg immediately woke up. He said, "What in the world was I dreaming? This can't happen ever!" Larry, Jr. picked up the phone and hollered from the living room, "It's your ex-wife, Greg." Greg answered the phone and asked her to call back later. Larry, Jr. stood in the doorway and said, "I am out of here, man. See you later." Greg sat there sweating with his eyes wide opened. Larry, Jr. asks, "Man, what's wrong with you?" Greg replied, "Nothing man. I had a crazy dream." Larry, Jr. said, "She must have been one fine woman, got you sweating like that." Larry, Jr. left out of the house and walked home.

A car pulled up. It was Bryan. He asked Larry, Jr. if he wanted a ride and Larry, Jr. got into the car. Bryan asked him had he heard anything else about his sister's situation. Larry stated that he did not want to talk about it right now. While they were talking, Larry, Jr. spotted Tyler in a crowd of guys shooting dice. Tyler was squat down, laughing and grabbing the money off the concrete pointing at the guys around him. Then Tyler saw Larry, Jr. and stood up as he passed by in an all black, gold trimmed Cadillac with chrome spinning rims. Larry, Jr. points out of the window at Tyler. Tyler stretched out his arms and smiles at Larry, Jr. Bryan asked, "What was all that about?" Larry, Jr. did not respond to the question from Bryan. When he arrived at the apartment, there was a car in the driveway. It was Larry, Sr. sitting in the car crying with his head hung down. Larry, Jr. was wondering why he was there, as he got out of Bryan's car. Larry, Jr. opens the door and goes into the apartment, leaving Larry, Sr. outside in the car. Larry, Sr. eventually knocks at the door and goes in. He sat down in the chair at the kitchen table with his head down with tears gliding down his face.

Larry, Jr. asked, "Man, why are you here? We don't need you here now. Maybe if you had been around more. Man, whatever, just leave." Larry, Sr. lifts up his head and screams, "I never wanted you, your mother or sister to be hurt by my sick life, but I chose to be gay over supporting and raising my family. Is it so wrong to just be free to be me? Is it? Son, tell me what can I do to make it all better, tell me," he says crying and shouting, trying to get Larry, Jr. to see it from his point of view.

Larry, Jr. turned to his dad and said, "It never mattered that you are gay, dad. It mattered that you were not there! You being the way you are is your choice. That does not determine who I am going to be, but whether gay or straight, raising your children should always come first. A child loves their parent no matter what they are as long as they are there and care for them. My mother is a single black woman raising her children alone, taking you back and forth to court in order for you to take care of your children. The pressure of life is pounding and pounding her every day. She working late hours, double shifts, hitching rides, and walking in the cold at night to support us. And I have to sit and watch her go through not knowing what to do, but to say words to encourage her and kiss her on the forehead so she knows this man got her back. Now my babysitter is lying in the hospital and I don't know whether or not she is going to make it or not. So you sit here wanting me to feel sorry for you. You made your choice ten years ago when my mom and I walked in on you and your secret lover, whoever he was. I advise you to leave before I catch two cases."

As Larry, Sr. stood on his feet, the door unlocked. It was Loraine coming into the house. She saw Larry, Sr. and she stated, "Not today, Larry, Sr. I am not up for it." He looked at her with one tear in his eye and asked, "How is she?" "She is still out," Loraine replied. He dug into his pocket and spread five one hundred dollar bills onto the dinning room table and replied, "There will be more and left." Loraine asked Larry Jr. what that was all about. He lifted up his shoulders and walked into his room. He came back into the kitchen where his mother was and he said, "I know who done this to Kimmie. I think I am going to have a little talk with him today. Also, Kimmie's friend, Theresa, she had something to do with it. Tyler's boys said that she sold Kimmie out for twenty five dollars worth of crack. Yes, Theresa smokes crack, her and her mama. That's why he runs things over there. But he will not run anything over here at the Peterson's house." As he was reaching for his coat to put around him onto his shoulders, a nine millimeter black gun fell out of his pocket.

Loraine replied, "What are you planning on doing with that gun, Larry, Jr.? So you tell me you want me to have one child in a coma and the other one in jail or dead. Is this how it ends? As hard as I work and try to live right, this is what you two have learned from me. There are too many of us single mothers seeing our children stolen by the devil and his tricks. We have given all that we know how to make sure you all made the right choices in life. For you to live in my house, see my struggles, and all the young people who lost their life, what is wrong with you boy!"

Larry, Jr. stood there with so much anger inside of him. He replied to his mother, "I am tired of different men coming into your life trying to destroy you and I cannot do anything about it. No, mom, you don't have men in and out of your bed, but when something needs to be repaired the handyman charges you twice as much, or when you go to get your car fixed because you are a woman they think you're stupid because they fix one thing and tamper with another so you keep coming back. They know you are a single woman. How about your boss on your job keep making you do double shifts or extra work because you want sleep with him because he knows you need your job and have two children and no man. As a man, mom, how do you think I feel? Now my sister is in the hospital because some punk thinks he can get away with this! This is one man I can stop and will stop!"

Loraine reaches for Larry, Jr. and he snatches away from her and slams the door behind him. Loraine fell to the floor and began to shout out, "Lord, I need You right now!" Then there was a knock at the door and Loraine jumped up it was Vanessa. She had on a long black coat with big white round sunglasses on. She asked Loraine was she ok. Loraine wiped her face, sat at the table and began to tell Vanessa what was going on and that Kimmie's condition was the same. When Vanessa removed her glasses, she had bruises around her eyes, on her neck and arms. She told Loraine that she caught Bryan again with another woman. She stated that, "He followed my car back home. As I was entering the house, I felt him punch me in my back so hard I fell into the house. He then twisted my hair around his fist and pulled me up onto my feet. I asked him not to hit me. That he could do whatever he wanted. I did not care if he had someone else. He beat me until I passed out. When I woke up he was stood over me with the broom and dust pan asking me to clean up the mess. After I swept the floor and bent over to pick up the trash, he kicked me in the face. Then he left and said he'll be back when he gets back. So I went upstairs, cleaned myself up and came over to see you." Loraine asked did she want to go to the hospital. Vanessa said, "No, if he found out I went anywhere, he'd kill me." Loraine fixed both of them some coffee and they sat on the couch talking about life, how women go through so much. Loraine said, "We are the ones who are titled as high risk in heart diseases, high risk in Aids testing. Why we always have to be the ones high in the negative stuff? Why not highest to be CEO of a billion dollar corporation? How about the highest to make it in Congress, a whole gang of us in the White House? Loraine and Vanessa began to laugh out loud. "So many times I thought about leaving and just starting all over again, but I thought who was going to raise my kids. I did not want anybody touching on my daughter or my son. Girl, I just don't know." They both fell asleep, one on the couch and the other on the love chair. Then the phone rang it was Pastor Love checking to see if it was it okay for him to come over. Loraine told him he could come over. Vanessa said that she was going home because she did not want Pastor Love to see her in that condition. Loraine went to take a shower for some peace of mind. She began to sang, pray to God for strength and ask Him to protect her children. She said, "Lord, I know no weapon formed against me shall prosper, no not a one." And she started to laugh inside of herself. As she exited out of the shower, Loraine heard police car sirens and ambulances passing her apartment with flashing lights. Then there was a knock at the door and her phone ranged at the same time. She ran to the door as she opened the door, her towel fell at her feet. Pastor Love and one of the deacons stood at the door, but the deacon's back was turned looking out at the streets seeing where the police were going. Pastor Love grabbed Loraine to cover her and she reaches for her towel. She is apologizing the whole time and Pastor Love knows that she has a lot of things going on. The phone rang again. It was the hospital informing her to come there immediately. She ran into her bedroom grabbed some sweats, t-shirt and flip flops. She asked Pastor Love and the deacon if they knew what happened. She told them about her conversation with Larry, Jr. as they headed out of the apartment into the car to the hospital.

When Loraine got to the hospital, she was met by Lisa and one of the doctors. Loraine asked, "How is Kimmie? Did she come through? Somebody please tell me something!" The doctor then turned and said, "Mrs. Peterson, you were not called here for your daughter, but for your son. He was shot seven times—twice in the face, twice in the chest, once in the back, once in the neck and in the stomach. There is severe bleeding and I really do not think he will make it. I am sorry, but it will take a miracle if he comes through." Loraine fainted and Pastor Love caught her in his arms and carried her to an empty room. After a few hours, she woke up and Pastor Love was sitting next to her. He informed her that Kimmie had come out of her coma and some of her tests were negative. Loraine got up, but was a little dizzy Pastor Love told her to wait a few moments before she got up. The doctor entered the room and told her that it was ok to see Kimmie now. Loraine asked Pastor Love what about Larry, Jr. he told her that her son was in surgery. She eased off of the bed, placed her feet on the floor and began to walk. When she went into Kimmie's room it was like this cloud of peace came over her. Loraine felt as though an elephant had been lifted off of her shoulders, but in her heart it felt empty. Kimmie asked where were her big brother? Nobody said anything and Loraine changed the subject. She asked, "Kimmie, some of your tests came back. Did the doctors tell you anything?" Kimmie replied, "Mom, I know you are trying to hide something, so what is it?"

Loraine said, "Now is not the time, ok baby, you just get better." Kimmie said that they had not told her any news about her tests. Loraine called for the nurse to come in. The nurse informed them that Kimmie was H.I.V. positive and that she had much heroine in her system that she may become addicted if not continually treated. Kimmie screamed out, "Why me, mom!" Loraine held her so tight and told her everything will be alright. Pastor Love told Loraine to ask the doctor for something to calm Kimmie down as the nurse was going out of the room. The doctor and nurses ran down the hallway passed Kimmie's room. Loraine stood in the room doorway they were racing to someone, which was Larry Jr. She saw a young man laying there fighting for his life. One of the nurses came up to her and said, "Mrs., please leave, you should not be here." With tears in her eyes, Loraine slowly walked away. Pastor Love had stood at the other end of the hallway. He opened his arms, hugged her, and she cried while they stood there. One of the nurses that work with Loraine told her she could go in with her son only for a moment. She went into the room alone with Larry, Jr. and he turned and looked at his mother. He said, "Mom, I love you and Kimmie always. I never dreamed my life would end like this." He started to cough. Loraine said, "Son, you don't have to say anything and we love you too. What happened?" Larry, Jr. replied, "I went to shoot Tyler, but I couldn't so I went to my friend Greg's house just to have someone to talk to. When I knocked at the door it took him a long time to answer. So I heard feet running, he opened the door, and I asked was someone there, if so I could come back later on. He was like "no that's okay Larry, Jr. come on in." While I was talking to him I saw a shadow under the door in his room. I looked in the corner by the sofa and there was dad's coat and hat. So I leaped up and kicked the bedroom door opened. He was laid on the bed with no shirt on. I told him my sister is in the hospital fighting for her life and you're here doing this. Then I pulled out my gun, pointed in his face. Mom, I told him he was not even worth it. Now I left there mad and the guy who told me about Tyler points me out to Tyler. So they started chasing me and I duck into the corner store. When I walked out, that's all I can remember."

Larry, Jr. started to cough more and gasped for air. Loraine hollered for the nurses to come see about her son. The nurse came in and started calling for the doctor and other nurses to assist her. Loraine was asked to leave the room. The monitor was beeping, the lines were up and down then his heart rate had dropped, the monitor showed a straight line. The doctor dropped his head and the nurses that worked with Loraine started crying as they covered him and walked away from his bedside.

Loraine was sitting on the floor outside of his room, her knees pressed against her chest, with rolls and rolls of tears sliding down her face. When she turned and looked at the doorway, she saw footsteps coming out of Larry, Jr.'s room.

The doctor and nurses came out of Larry, Jr.'s room. The doctor pulled the mask off his face, as he sat down in front of her and said, "I am so sorry, Mrs. Peterson, we lost him. We tried everything in our power to keep your son alive." She reached out her arms and grabbed his coat and screamed out, "Why?"

Pastor Love heard her and came running down the hall out of Kimmie's room. He stood over her as she looked up at him. She asked him, "Why did this have to happen to me, Pastor? What have I done so wrong for me to have both of my children in the hospital at the same time just down the hall from each other, one with AIDS, who could also be a drug addict. My only son has died for nothing. Pastor, tell me why. I have lived my life the best way I knew how. I go to church every time the doors open. I work very, very hard to provide for my children. I taught them the ways that are righteous; constantly praying over, over and over for God to watch over them," shouting and screaming at Pastor Love with tears flowing down her face Loraine continued to stumble over her words. She reached her hands out to him, wanting to know, why this was happening to her.

Pastor Love snatched her up next to him. Holding her close he whispered in her ear, "This too shall pass." Loraine held him even more tightly as they walk away from Larry, Jr.'s room.

The male nurses rolled Larry, Jr.'s body down the hall in the opposite direction. Pastor Love told Loraine, "Maybe you should go home for a while to get some rest. Then come back tomorrow to see Kimmie because she doesn't need to see you like this. I will come and check on you sometime tomorrow, okay? I will call a taxi to pick you up and I'll tell Kimmie I told you to go get some rest." Loraine did not put up a fight, but just nodded her head and got into the taxi. While riding in the car, Loraine fell asleep. When the taxi driver woke her up, she was in front of her apartment door. She thanked the driver and offered to pay him, but Pastor Love had already taken care of the fare. She opened the door to her apartment. It was cold and quiet. Loraine went into Larry, Jr.'s room and stretched out on his bed.

Reality Check:

The storms have to end in life. Trouble doesn't last always. I was once told, "Do not make a long-term decision in a temporary situation." If you give up now, who will fight for your children and your children's children? This is the good fight of faith. Trust and believing in the Lord Almighty no matter what comes or goes. Although we may not understand some situations in our life, it does not mean that God cannot recognize them. Nothing surprises God. He knows all about our troubles. Loraine has come to a crossroad in her life and so will you. Remember, the Savior is with you to keep you and to deliver you.

Enemies

"But I say unto you which hear; Love your enemies, do good to them which hate you... and pray for them which despitefully use you" (Luke 6:27, 28 KJV).

~ Enemies ~

Early in the morning, Loraine arose onto her feet. She made herself a cup of coffee and stood in front of her kitchen window looking outside. It was raining. The wind was blowing and the sun was out. She held tight to her hot cup of coffee and her warm thick rose colored robe.

The phone rang. It was Vanessa informing her that she was on her way over and for Loraine to open the door because of the pouring rain. Loraine was sitting on the couch when Vanessa arrived. Vanessa took off her dripping wet rain coat, hugged Loraine, and sat down beside her. She could see that Loraine's eyes were swollen and bloodshot red from crying all night. Loraine offered Vanessa some coffee. As they drank it, Vanessa asked, "Loraine, I know you don't want to talk about this right now. When do you think you will be able to start thinking about funeral arrangements? If I can be of any assistance, please let me know." Loraine looked at her and said, "Vanessa, how can I even think of my son's funeral now! I haven't even told Kimmie her brother is dead. I still cannot believe that he is gone. If you want to, you plan the funeral yourself!" Loraine had become distressed with Vanessa. She quickly apologized to her for her actions.

Vanessa tried to change the conversation by asking about Loraine and Pastor Love. Vanessa asked, "Pastor Love has been hanging in there with you, Loraine. What's going on with you two? Some of the people are talking about how much time he has been spending with you and that there are other families in the church having crisis too you know. It seems like you are first priority nowadays." Loraine turned and looked at her and said, "Are you here to cheer me up or add to my problems because if you are, you can just leave. I thought I was being rude to you; now you just being stupid all together. You can take it personal. I really don't care how you receive it, but get out of my apartment, now! You about to make me lose my mind up in here!" Loraine pointing her finger at the door as Vanessa grabs her things. "They said you find out who your friends are when you're down. All you can come in here with is gossip about what people are saying about me and Pastor Love. I want to know what your part was in the conversation." Walking behind Vanessa with her hand on her hip and constantly pointing her finger at Vanessa. "Are you trying to find out something so you can tell the people something? Get out of here now!" Vanessa grabbed her coat and said, "I hope somebody else gets him before your sorry self does." Loraine shouted out the door, "I hope your husband knocks your eyes out of your head the next time," and she threw her coffee cup at her car. Loraine went back into the apartment and slammed her door.

As she was in the bathroom getting dressed, she heard a knock at the door. It was Larry, Sr. and Greg. They had heard about Larry, Jr. and wanted to explain to Loraine what had happened. She said, "I do not want to hear nothing you two have to say. I do not even want to see your faces. Please leave!" They headed for the door and she slammed it after them. Loraine asked, "What is this 'rain on Loraine' week? If somebody else comes to my door, I will scream." There was a knock and she screamed.

When she opened the door it was Pastor Love standing there smiling at her. She began to laugh. He was wondering why she was laughing. "I am here to take you to the hospital to see Kimmie. Are you ready?" he asked. She said, "I just need to finish putting on my clothes." He said, "Loraine, come here for a minute" she sat on the couch beside him. "I know that you feel as though life has given you the rough end, but just trust that God will make everything alright again, okay?" She leaned over and said, "Pastor, I know that everything happens for a reason. I was thinking to myself last night, I have done my best raising my children and I cannot stop them from making good or bad decisions. I can only advise them to make the best ones. The rest was up to them. Pastor,

I do not know where my son is, but I pray that he is with our heavenly Father. I know one thing, I loved my son and still love my daughter." He reached to hug her, but their lips met and they kissed. She pulled away stared at him and he stared back. They continued to kiss. He picked her up into his arms and placed her in his lap. Loraine started taking his shirt off. She stood up, took him by the hand, and led him toward her bedroom. He stopped, stared at her in the doorway of her bedroom while she was letting her hair down. He then whispered in her ear, "I can't stop myself from wanting you any longer." Then he entered into her bedroom. When they stood there, Loraine replied, "Please take me and make love to me just this one time if never again." They were standing face to face when he swept her off her feet and laid her on the bed.

The phone rang. It was the police department. They caught Tyler and his friends that morning. The police officer wanted her to come and identify the people who shot her son. She told Pastor Love that she had to go to the police department and if he wanted, he could stay there until she returned. He asked her if would she be okay. She said she would be fine and that she would take a cab. He kissed her so she got up, dressed, then left.

When Loraine arrived, she saw Tyler standing in the line-up smiling. Loraine told the detective that he was the one. The detective told her that they had waited a long time to arrest him, but he kept slipping through the system. When they dismissed the men from the line up, their lawyers were waiting outside for them. Tyler walked out and went to his attorney who was Bryan, Vanessa's husband. Loraine's heart hit the bottom of her stomach. She rushed over to them both and said, "Bryan, how could you? Out of all the people to defend you have to choose my son's murderer. What kind of person are you?"

Bryan replied, "The kind of man that does not get business twisted. So don't come over here, Mrs. Righteous, trying to mess up my cash flow. Your son should have been in his place and maybe none of this would have happened. Now if there is nothing else I can assist you with, me and my client are on our way to lunch. Do you want to come?" Bryan laughed as he and Tyler walked away. Loraine reached onto one of the officer's desk, grabbed a stapler and hit Tyler on the back of the head. Two police officers grabbed her and three others held Tyler as he turned to punch her. Bryan started shouting, "My client will press charges. You have done it now!" The detective tried to calm Loraine down. He said, "Mrs. Peterson, please go home and let us handle this." Loraine left the police station and was on her way home.

Pastor Love was still in the bed sleep when he felt hands rubbing him on his chest and back. Then he moved when he felt kissing and nibbling on his ears. He turned and said, "You know that's my weak spot." And a voice said, "So it is." Pastor Love hopped up in the bed. It was Vanessa lying beside him with no clothes on. Pastor Love replied, "Vanessa, what are you doing? Stop touching me." Vanessa flipped on top of him holding his arms down. She stated, "Oh, Pastor Love is working with a whole lot of love. I knew you were doing her just like you did me. Who is better me or her, Pastor? How many have you done, Mr. Love?" Pastor Love replied, "It is not like that with Loraine I care about her. It was nothing with you, I mean nothing. Your husband tried to kill me over nothing. Now I am only going to ask you once again. Get off of me!" He began wrestling with her and threw her onto the floor. He landed on top of her. He said, "Get out of here before I hurt you. You mean nothing to me. I love Loraine." After he said that, Loraine walked into the room with tears in her eyes and her umbrella in her hand. She started swinging it at both of them. Vanessa reached for her clothes and Pastor Love wass trying to explain to her. He wass holding both of Loraine's arms, asking her to please calm down so he can talk to her. Vanessa ran out of the apartment with her dress and shoes in her hand and wearing only her black slip. As she ran out, Byran was coming up the stairs to confront Loraine about what happened at the police station, but he caught Vanessa running out of the apartment undressed. Byran said to her, "Go home before I kill you right here where you stand." She tried to explain to him, but he yelled at her, "Now!"

Loraine told Pastor Love to leave and he stood in front of the door with his arms stretched in front of her and he said, "Loraine, please listen to me. How could I tell you something like that? I never knew that my feelings for you would grow this strong. Please give me a chance. What do you want me to do, just tell me? With tears in her eyes, Loraine said, "Just leave. There is nothing you can say or do for me ever again, Pastor Love. I gave you my soul, body and mind to protect and love. I have given you something that no man has had in over ten years. When I did give myself to someone, I wanted it to be with someone special and I thought you were that special somebody. I have learned one thing. You can't turn to your best friends because they'll screw you. Now I can't even turn to my Pastor because he's screwing me too. Now Pastor Love, you tell me who do you turn to when all else has failed?"

Pastor Love replied, "Loraine, you might feel that everything is going wrong now, but never forget you can always turn to God and trust in Him because we can't get mad at Him for life's disappointments. He gives us all free will so the question is what are we willing to do? Loraine, I love you so much. I have never felt like this for any woman. Please baby, give me another chance. I am on my knees begging you." She turned to him, held him, and rubbed his head against her stomach. Her tears were falling onto his back.

Pastor Love stood to his feet, kissed her on her forehead, and left. Loraine leaned against the door looking out of the window, with her eyes overflowing with water and lips trembling. She wondered what else she could take before the pressures of life pounded her into pieces. Loraine thought to herself, "What is it about me that I have to encounter so much in my life? I know of people that have been through things, but nothing like what I am going through. Maybe I should just give up all together. The harder I worked to keep my family together, it just fell apart. Did I spend enough time with my children? Should I have left them and just start my life over alone? They probably would have been better off than here with me. What will people think about me? I cannot show my face at the church. The members are already talking. Once they find out about me sleeping with the Pastor, they will think I got what I deserved.

Loraine went into the bathroom, looked in the mirror at herself, and cried, while she pulled her hair out of her face. She opened the medicine cabinet, reached for the bottle of pain medication, and poured twenty pills into her hand. She stared at herself in the mirror for two minutes, then took the pills and smeared them in the mirror.

Loraine spoke to herself, "I won't give up. It is not over yet." I still have a daughter to fight for and my life to live. Now I have raised those kids the best way I knew how. I cannot change the things that have already happened, but I can prepare for the things to come. Now Loraine, you got to get yourself together. That thing with Pastor Love is something that happened in your vulnerable state. You are a single woman who will live to tell the story of how you overcame."

"I will not die!" She went in her room, turned on her gospel and picked out some night clothes, with dried up tears in her eyes. Loraine ran some bath water in the tub with candles all around. She sat in the tub covered with white fluffy bubbles all over her. In her right hand was a glass of wine and in the other, she held the wine bottle. She got out of the tub, dried off, and went to bed.

Then the phone rang. It was Pastor Love on the other end. He wanted to know if she was okay and if she had a chance to see Kimmie. Loraine laid in the bed with the telephone cord wrapped around her little finger as she talked to him. He asked if she was ready to start making the funeral arrangements. She told him that she was, so they began to make some of the preparations. Once everything was covered, he said good night to Loraine. She replied good night also to him and they paused for a moment, then they hung up.

Revive

"Though I walk in the mist of trouble,
thou wilt revive me..."
(Psalms 138:7).

~ Revive ~

Loraine laid across the bed as the morning sun shined on her face from the window over her bed. She got up, went into the bathroom, washed her face, and grabbed some clothes to wear to the hospital.

Loraine arrived at the hospital to see Kimmie. She ran into Lisa in the hallway. Loraine asked her how she was doing and why was she at the hospital. Lisa told Loraine that she had not been feeling well. She said she had been vomiting, was dizzy, and had bad headaches. The doctor did a pregnancy test and she was waiting on the results.

Loraine smiled at her and said, "Sounds like you might be pregnant, girl." The nurse came out informed Lisa that her test result was positive. Lisa stared at Loraine with a far away look and replied, "Mrs. Peterson, I can't be pregnant! I only had sex once! How can this be? We used a condom. We were so careful!" She started to cry and Loraine held her and said, "Well, you are going to have to tell whoever the baby's father is about this. Lisa pulls away from Loraine and holds her head down. She said, "Mrs. Peterson, I can't because the father is dead. Larry, Jr. was my baby's daddy." Loraine asked, when this happened? I've never seen you two together. Lisa, are you sure?" Lisa replied, "Yes! It was my first time, my only time." she said, with tears running down her face. "Loraine, I would never say something like this at a time like this. We can have a blood test if you want to!" Loraine said to her, "Don't worry about all that, I believe you. Let's go see Kimmie now."

They entered the room. Kimmie's doctor was in the room also. He told Loraine that he was discharging Kimmie. Then he told her to not be concerned about the heroin addiction because they got the remaining dose out of her system, to make sure she takes her medication properly and she or the baby will not have any problems. He informed Loraine that even though Kimmie had the disease, it may not pass to her unborn child. Kimmie got dressed and Loraine headed down the hall to go home with her daughter and Lisa.

The taxi dropped them off at the apartment door and Loraine opened the door for Kimmie and Lisa. Then Kimmie asked where Larry, Jr. was and why she had not seen him at the hospital. Lisa looked at Loraine with water-filled eyes as if she was wondering what Loraine was going to say to her. Loraine asked Kimmie to sit down for a moment. Then she began to tell her everything that happened, even what Lisa had told her earlier in the hospital. While she was talking to her, tears slid down Kimmie's face, then she jumped up, ran into the bathroom, and started vomiting. When she came out of the bathroom she asked when the funeral would be held. Loraine said, "The funeral is tomorrow Kimmie, but if you do not feel up to it you do not have to attend." Kimmie replied, "How can I not attend my own brother's funeral, mom!" Loraine said, "Please, Kimmie, do not get yourself upset. I just thought with you being pregnant it might be too stressful for you." Kimmie said, "No, mom, I'll be okay."

Lisa told Kimmie she would see them later or at the funeral. She was going home to tell her mother about her pregnancy. Loraine went into Larry, Jr.'s room and Kimmie followed after her. They both stretched out on his bed, talking about the things they all had done in the past. Loraine remembered when Larry, Jr. was about six-years-old, when she woke up one morning, she entered the kitchen and he was standing on a chair with pancake mix all over him and a bowl in his hand. He had dishes everywhere. She asked him what was he doing and he said he was cooking her breakfast for her to go back to bed. Kimmie started laughing and cried at the same time. She rolled over toward her mother held her, while both of them cried. They both fell asleep on Larry Jr.'s bed.

There was silence in the apartment for the first time in a long time. Loraine woke up late that night with dried tears on her face. She walked into her room to call Pastor Love. He answered the phone after the first ring. Loraine paused for a few moments, and then she said, "Hello, Pastor Love, I am calling about the remaining touches on the funeral arrangements for my son." He replied, "Loraine, what do you want done and thank you for calling. I was getting worried about you and Kimmie." Loraine stated, "I just want to keep this on a Pastor and member basis only please. I need to start getting things in order for my family, alone." Then Pastor Love said, "If that's how you want it, okay. Explain to me how you want everything and I'll give the rest of the information to Sister Midway tomorrow." Loraine responded, "Thank you for everything, Pastor." Pastor love said, "Wait Loraine!" He asked her, "How can we just forget what happened? How do we get over or even handle this, Loraine? Maybe you can brush what happened to the side, but I cannot!" Loraine said, "I would like to thank you again for everything, Pastor." She then hung up the phone and went into her closet to pick out something for her son's funeral.

While she looked through her closet, she reminisced about Larry, Jr. and what he told her. Loraine got up that morning with hardly any rest on the day of her son's funeral. She stood in front of her bedroom mirror as she slipped on her silky pleated black dress that zipped up in the back. She slid her stockings on with tears still gliding down her face. She stepped into her black heels with a sparkling diamond pendent on top. Kimmie was dressed when Loraine came down the hall. They hugged each other, wiped their faces and smiled as they walked toward the kitchen. Loraine and Kimmie were sitting at the table with breakfast on the table, but neither one of them ate anything.

The telephone was constantly ringing back to back, but neither one of them moved. Then, there was a loud knock at the door. Loraine slid her chair from the table and stood up while brushing her dress off trying to get herself together. When she opened the door, it was Vanessa standing there with a raincoat and tears coming down her face. Loraine slammed the door in her face, walked back to the table and looked straight at Kimmie. Vanessa knocked at the door continually, louder and louder. Kimmie leaped up fast-paced walking toward the door. When she opened the door, Bryan was dragging Vanessa down the steps by her hair. Blood was on the door, on the outside steps. Kimmie screamed out to Loraine. "Mom!" Loraine went to the door and stood there looking as Bryan dragged Vanessa into the street while cars were coming. Kimmie cried out, "Mommy, please do something, make him stop!"

Loraine then ran out into the street after them and jumped on Bryan's back. Kimmie ran to call the police for help. Bryan grabbed Loraine and threw her onto the concrete sidewalk. Vanessa hit Bryan on the back with a stick she picked up off the ground. He fell flat on the ground as Vanessa and Loraine stood over him. The police came up; handcuffed him, and took him down to the police station. Vanessa turned to Loraine and said, "Thank you so much. I have no way of thanking you enough for what you have done. Loraine, please can you find it in your heart to forgive me?" Loraine turned and walked away while straightening out her dress and looked back and said, "I can forgive, but I can't forget." The funeral limo had arrived as she was walking toward her apartment. Kimmie ran over and told Loraine she gave the officers all the information. They headed for the funeral in the long, shiny, black, Chrysler 300 limo.

Forgiveness

"For if you forgive men their trespasses, your Heavenly Father will also forgive you." But if ye forgive not men their trespasses neither will your Father forgive your trespasses."
Matthew 6:14, 15 KJV

~ Forgiveness ~

The church parking lot was filled with hundreds of people who were standing in a line outside. There were hundreds sitting inside as well. When Kimmie and her mother arrived, they were surprised at how many people were there. Loraine rolled down the window with her head out and her mouth wide open. She turned to Kimmie and shook her head. The driver asked Loraine if they were they ready to go in and she replied, "Yes." So he went around the limo to open the door for her and her daughter. As they walked up the sidewalk holding hands, with their heads held up, people said how sorry they were for their loss.

When they walked in the church everybody stood up with tears in their eyes. The ushers escorted them to the front of the church to view the body. Loraine closed her eyes and began to pray to God. She said, "Lord, help me to get over all that has happened to my family. Sometimes I wonder if You are with me. I was so mad because of what happened to my son. He was a good boy. Lord, why take him? Was it something I did? Lord, if you are with me, send me a sign.

Just give me the strength to go on and have no hatred in my heart toward anybody. Loraine Peterson shall go forth in Jesus name." The choir stood up to sing when Pastor Love entered the pulpit. He looked down at Kimmie and Loraine with glassy eyes and a small bright smile. They both smiled back at him with the same glassy eyes. Loraine looked down on the floor. When she looked back up to her left it was Larry, Sr. with Greg. They were walking toward her, so she sat back in her seat with a straight face. Larry, Sr. stood over her and said, "Loraine, I don't know what to say, but I was wrong for everything. Please! Can you ever forgive me for the hurt and pain I have caused you?" She lifted up her head and said, "Yes, you have caused me and my children much hurt, but staying mad with you will not bring him back. So I have forgiven you and you, Greg," Loraine stated, letting them know that she knew what had happen. "I was very angry with myself and others, but God still has something better in store for Mrs. Peterson. I will not let anything or anyone stop me now. You can go, Larry, Sr. in peace because I sincerely have forgiven you." He thanked her and they returned back to their seats. Pastor Love ministered and then asked if the family had remarks. Kimmie went up to speak. She said, "Larry, Jr. was my big brother, I love him and he always protected me. Mom would tell me not to and I did, but he still loved me and kept on protecting me from myself. I will always love you, Larry, Jr., no matter what." Loraine went up to give her remarks as well. While she gave her remarks, Pastor Love came up to her. He asked her would she forgive him for what he had done to her. Pastor Love stood there with tears in his eyes then bent down on one knee and asked her would she marry him with a sparkling marquee cut, three-carat diamond ring in his hand. She looked at him with a puzzled expression thinking within herself why is he asking me this at my son's funeral. It sounds like someone was calling her from far-off, saying, Mom! Mom! Mom! Loraine immediately felt faint. She passed out and hit her head on the floor, "Bam!" When she woke up, she screamed, "Larry, Jr., where are you?" But Kimmie, Vanessa and Pastor Love stood over her. Then she looked at the foot of the chair that she was laid on, sitting there with her was Larry, Jr. He stood up, walked in front of her, and kneeled down beside her, staring into his mother's eyes. He said, "Mom, here I am."

She looked at everybody and asked what happened, what's going on? She replied, "I thought that you were dead, Larry Jr., and Kimmie are you pregnant?" She sat up in the chair with an astounded look in her eyes. She looked at Pastor Love, asked him "Did we?" while pointing back and forth at Pastor Love and herself. Pastor Love laughed and replied, "No, Sister Peterson." Loraine got her thoughts together and rose up saying, "Thank God that it was all a dream!" She hugged her children extremely tight and screamed, "I love you two so much! Lord, I thank You for keeping this Woman and her children. Thank You!" Loraine experienced some hard times in her life it seemed. Life is hard and difficult without God, but with him all things are possible. When you have God in your life you can cast all your cares upon Him. I say to you no matter what comes or goes stand strong with Jesus and remember, Woman, Don't Die."

Reality Check

Have you ever had a dream that seemed so real? Even though it was a dream it still touched you in a way that it continues to bother you after you wake up. I can identify with Loraine. I have had dreams that I thanked God that they were not real. Just think about it, if God allowed some of those dreams to come true. How would we handle those situations in our life? Put yourself in Loraine's shoes. Believe it or not there are many Loraine Peterson out there in the world, Single Women that support their children alone pounding each and everyday to make ends meet, every woman desiring the best education, job, and spouse for their children. This is why she works hard, involves herself in higher education and builds a strong relationship with God first of all. She knows that no matter what, that God has her back. When you have this type of relationship, all things are possible through Christ Jesus. Remember that people will turn their backs on you in time of need. The Word of God tells us, "Put no trust in man." God is always there for us regardless of what is going on in our life. We must learn to commune with Him, talk with Him, walk with Him and always pray to Him. There is nothing too hard for God. He's got your back in a time of trouble. I pray that if we never meet, that God's voice is speaking to you in your situation right now. You need to know that there is no mountain too high, no valley too low and no sea too wide; that you're Heavenly Father can not reach you in a time of trouble. The everlasting Father will keep you in His perfect peace forever. If you have not received Christ as Lord and Savior, let this story be a testimony to you of how God can deliver you. We feel as if the pressures of life are consuming us, but Jesus wants us to cast our cares upon Him. Choose this day which master you will serve please let it be Jesus. Pick up a Bible read Romans 10:9 and confess all your sins to God because he is faithful to forgive you. Once you have decided God will be your Master and Lord over your life get with people that will speak life into your spirit. Then walk in the love and peace of God that He has given you. The Bible tells us, "Old things have passed away and behold new things are to come." He has cast your sins as far as the East is from the West. Now live a new life in Him and be blessed! Know that they overcame by their testimonies.

About the Author

Pastor Stephanie White is the wife of Rodney Lee White and the mother of five, also the grandmother of one. She has served in youth ministry, women ministry, outreach ministry and also assisted her Pastor. Pastor Stephanie White is the visionary of "Kingdom Business Ministry" in Hopewell, Virginia.

She is a student of Roanoke Seminary College in Elizabeth City North Carolina. She will graduate with her Bachelor in Divinity.

Pastor Stephanie White enjoys and has a passion for spreading the Good News of Jesus Christ. Her mission is to reach, teach and have compassion for people where they are in life. By the leading of the Holy Spirit she desires to win the lost Souls for Christ. Her favorite scriptures are Ephesians 6:10-11 "Finally brethren, be strong in the Lord, and in the power of his might. Put on the whole armour of God; that you may be able to stand against the wiles of the devil."

TO ORDER ADDITIONAL COPIES:

please forward your check or money order (plus shipping and handling) to:

Stephanie White
c/o "Woman, Don't Die"
29199 Meadowview Drive
Waverly, VA 23890
(e-mail) kbm249@hotmail.com
(website): facebook.com/ministerstephaniewhite

Qty.	Item	Unit Cost	Total
	Woman, Don't Die	15.95	
		Subtotal	
		Shipping	
		Grand Total	

SHIPPING & HANDLING: *Please add $3.00 shipping for each item ordered. For orders placed outside of the U.S., add $6.00 shipping per item.*

Ship to: ____

______________________ ______________________ **(Mr./Mrs./Ms.)**________
Last Name **First Name**

____
Street Address

______________________________, ______________ ________
City **State** **Zip**

Phone: (   )______________________ **Email:**______________________

Thank you for placing your order.